b small publishing

FRENCH FUN

**Bonjour, je suis française.
Je m'appelle Marie.**
boh-*shoor*, sh' swee froh-*sez*
sh' ma*pell* Ma*ree*
Hello, I'm French.
My name is Marie.

**Hello, I'm English.
My name is Peter.**
Bonjour, je suis anglais.
Je m'appelle Peter.
boh-*shoor* sh' sweez on-*gleh*
sh' ma*pell* Peter

Catherine Bruzzone
and Lone Morton

Illustrations by Louise Comfort

bonjour
boh-*shoor*
hello

au revoir
oh r'v*wah*
goodbye

bonsoir
boh-*swah*
good evening

bonne nuit
bon nwee
goodnight

salut
sal*oo*
hi

✂

bonjour

bonjour

au revoir

au revoir

bonsoir

bonsoir

bonne nuit

bonne nuit

salut

salut

Bonjour…

Cut out the French words below. Put them in the speech bubbles and practise the different greetings. Read them aloud.

Keep the words and you can play the game again.

First write in your name and age. Then fill in the correct ages in French below and read them aloud.

Je m'appelle _____

J'ai _____ ans.

12

8

J'ai _____ ans.

J'ai _____ ans.

2

5

7

J'ai _____ ans.

J'ai _____ ans.

J'ai _____ ans.

Je m'appelle…
sh'map-*el*
My name is…

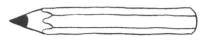

J'ai … ans.
shay … ahn
I am … years old.

1	**un**	ahn
2	**deux**	der
3	**trois**	trwah
4	**quatre**	catr'
5	**cinq**	sank
6	**six**	seess
7	**sept**	set
8	**huit**	weet
9	**neuf**	nerf
10	**dix**	deess
11	**onze**	ohz
12	**douze**	dooz
13	**treize**	trez
14	**quatorze**	cat-*orz*
15	**quinze**	canz
16	**seize**	sehz
17	**dix-sept**	dees-*set*
18	**dix-huit**	dees-*weet*
19	**dix-neuf**	dees-*nerf*
20	**vingt**	vahn

You'll find the numbers up to 100 on the inside cover.

Où est…?

oo eh

Where is…?

Où sont…?

oo soh

Where are…?

Read these questions aloud in French. Tick off the list when you have found each item.

Paris is the capital of France.

Où est Paris?

oo eh P*aree*

Where is Paris?

☐

Où sont les Alpes?

oo soh lez alp

Where are the Alps?

☐

Où est l'avion?

oo eh lavee*yoh*

Where is the plane?

☐

Où est le train?

oo eh ler trahn

Where is the train?

☐

Où sont les moutons?

oo soh leh moo*toh*

Where are the sheep?

☐

Où sont les vignobles?

oo soh leh veen*yobl'*

Where are the vineyards?

☐

Où sont les poissons?

oo soh leh pwa*soh*

Where are the fish?

☐

Où est…?

France is in Europe. It is bordered by six other European countries and three seas. Some of the names have been missed off this map. Can you fill them in, in English?

Answers and French pronunciation on the inside cover.

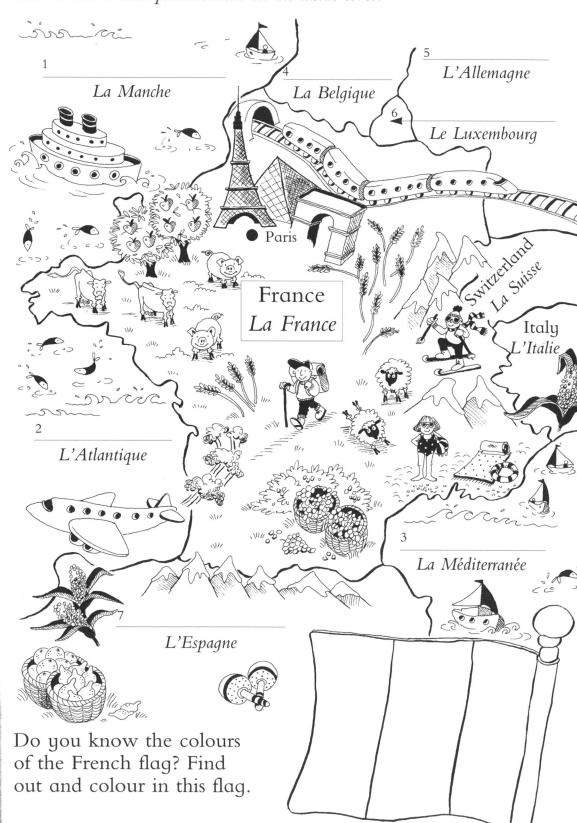

Do you know the colours of the French flag? Find out and colour in this flag.

Où est…?

Mark and Susan are lost. Can you help them find their way to the station? (*Answer on the inside cover.*)
Read the questions in the margin aloud in French.
Find each place on the map and then tick off the list.

Nous sommes perdus!
noo som pair*doo*
We are lost!

Où est la gare?
oo eh lah gar
Where is the station?

Où est le parc? ☐
oo eh ler par
Where is the park?

Où est l'école? ☐
oo eh le*col*
Where is the school?

Où est la poste? ☐
oo eh lah posst
Where is the post office?

Où est le cinéma?
oo eh ler seeneh-*mah* ☐
Where is the cinema?

Où est le restaurant?
oo eh ler resto-*roh* ☐
Where is the restaurant?

Où est le musée? ☐
oo eh ler moo*zeh*
Where is the museum?

Où est l'arrêt d'autobus? ☐
oo eh lar*reh* dotoboos
Where is the bus stop?

Où est le supermarché? ☐
oo eh ler supermar*sheh*
Where is the supermarket?

Où est l'église? ☐
oo eh leg-*leez*
Where is the church?

Où est la pharmacie? ☐
oo eh lah farmas*see*
Where is the chemist?

…s'il vous plaît
seel voo pleh
…please

5

Qu'est-ce que c'est?

Qu'est-ce que c'est?

kesker seh

What is it?

C'est…

seh

It's…

Ce sont…

ser soh

They are…

C'est une gomme.

set yoon gom

It's a rubber.

Ce sont des stylos.

ser soh deh stee*lo*

They are pencils.

C'est une table.

set yoon tah-bl'

It's a table.

C'est une règle.

set yoon rare-gl'

It's a ruler.

C'est un sac à dos.

set ahn sak ah doh

It's a rucksack.

Ce sont des livres.

ser soh deh leevr'

They are books.

Ce sont des ciseaux.

ser soh deh see*zo*

They are scissors.

C'est une chaise.

set yoon shez

It's a chair.

Qu'est-ce que c'est?

Join the dots to find out! Count in French as you go.
Then write the answers in French underneath.

The numbers from 21 to 100 and the answers are on the inside cover.

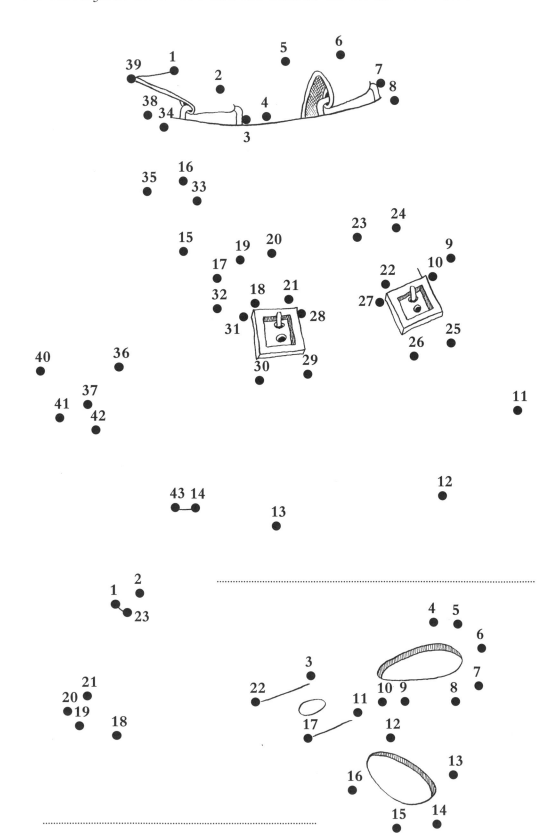

Match these up!

Match up these pictures, then practise saying the words aloud in French. You'll need two dice. Throw one die or two dice, as you like, and say the French name for the picture which corresponds to the number you threw.

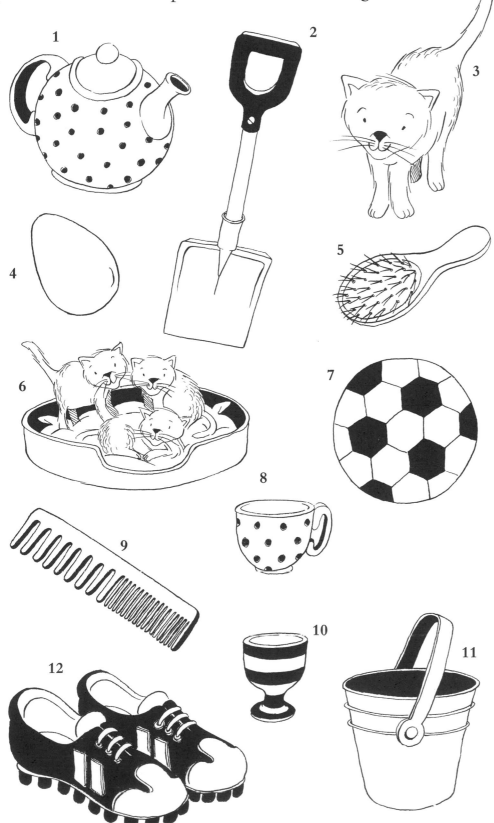

le peigne
ler peh-ny'
comb

le chat
ler shah
cat

le coquetier
ler koket*yeh*
egg cup

les chaussures de football
leh show-*sewer* der foot*bol*
football boots

les chatons
leh sha*toh*
kittens

la théière
lah ta*yair*
teapot

le seau
ler so
bucket

le ballon de football
ler bal*loh* der foot*bol*
football

l'œuf
lerf
egg

la tasse
la tass
cup

la pelle
la pell
spade

la brosse à cheveux
la bross ah sh'*ver*
hairbrush

7

J'aime…
shem
I like…

Je n'aime pas…
sh' nem pah
I don't like…

le soleil
ler so*lay*
sun

les poissons
leh pwas*soh*
fish

le château de sable
ler shat-*o* der sabl'
sandcastle

les vagues
leh vag
waves

les algues
lez alg
seaweed

le parasol
ler para*sol*
beach umbrella

la bouée de sauvetage
lah boo*eh* der sowv-*taj*
rubber ring

le crabe
ler krab
crab

les mouettes
leh moo-*ett*
seagulls

le ballon
ler bal*loh*
ball
8

J'aime…

Look at this beach scene and circle ten things you like.
Then say them out loud in French. Start with '**j'aime…**'.

le pull
ler pool
jumper

Les vêtements
leh *vet*moh
clothes

le chapeau
ler shap-*o*
hat

la robe
lah rob
dress

le pantalon
ler pont-er-*loh*
trousers

le maillot de bain
ler *my-o* der bahn
swimming costume

les chaussettes
leh show-*set*
socks

les chaussures
leh show-*sewer*
shoes

Cut carefully round these clothes to dress the characters.

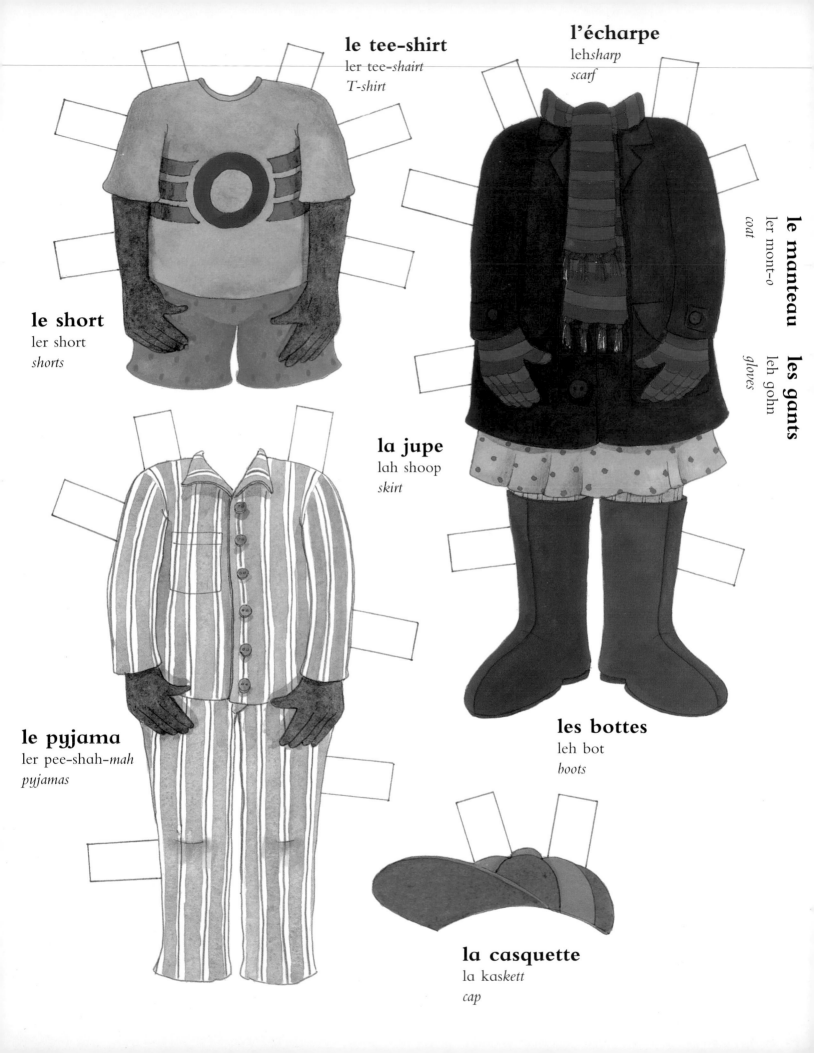

le tee-shirt
ler tee-*shairt*
T-shirt

l'écharpe
leh*sharp*
scarf

le short
ler short
shorts

le manteau
ler mont-o
coat

les gants
leh gohn
gloves

la jupe
lah shoop
skirt

le pyjama
ler pee-shah-*mah*
pyjamas

les bottes
leh bot
boots

la casquette
la kas*kett*
cap

Je n'aime pas…

Now circle four things you don't like. Say them out loud in French. Start with '**je n'aime pas…**'.

Combien de poissons?

combee-*yah* der pwass*oh*

How many fish?

How many fish can you find in the picture?

Answer on the inside cover.

le chapeau
ler shap-*o*
hat

la coquille
lah ko*kee*
shell

la plage
lah plaj
beach

la serviette
lah sair*viette*
towel

le voilier
ler vwalee-*eh*
sailing boat

le pique-nique
ler pic*neek*
picnic

le requin
ler re*kah*
shark

le maillot de bain
ler my-*o* der *bah*
swimsuit

la radio
lah radee*o*
radio

les lunettes de soleil
leh loo*nett* der solay
sunglasses

la méduse
lah med*yooz*
jellyfish

Combien?
combee-*yah*
How many?

9

la famille
lah fam-*ee*
family

la mère/maman
lah mair/mam*oh*
mother/mum

le père/papa
ler pair/pa*pa*
father/dad

la sœur
lah sir
sister

le frère
ler frair
brother

la grand-mère
lah groh-*mair*
grandmother

le grand-père
ler groh-*pair*
grandfather

le bébé
le beh-*beh*
baby

les parents
leh pah-*roh*
parents

la fille
lah fee
daughter

le fils
ler fees
son

les jumeaux
leh shoo-*mo*
twins

10

La famille

Match up the family members. Now label them in French. You may find there is more than one way to describe each person. *Answers on the inside cover.*

a

b

c

d

Le café

Practise ordering snacks in a café.
Play this game with a partner. Pretend you are ordering at this café. Use the picture to help you.
The first player orders, say '**un café, s'il vous plaît**'.
The next player repeats the order but adds something else, say '**un café et une glace, s'il vous plaît**'.
The winner is the last person to say the whole list correctly in the right order.

le café
ler ca*feh*
café/bar

une glace
yoon glas
ice-cream

un morceau de gâteau
ahn mor*so* der gat-*o*
a piece of cake

un café au lait
ahn ca*feh* o leh
a white coffee

un thé
ahn teh
a tea

un sandwich...
ahn sond-*weech*
a ... sandwich

...au jambon
o shom*boh*
...ham

...au fromage
o from*aj*
...cheese

un jus d'orange
ahn joo dor-*ronsh*
an orange juice

un chocolat chaud
ahn shoco*lah* show
a hot chocolate

un verre d'eau
ahn vair doh
a glass of water

C'est combien?
seh combee-*yah*
How much is it?

Je voudrais…
sh' vood-*reh*
I'd like…

le marché
ler marsh-*eh*
market

des tomates
deh to-*matt*
some tomatoes

des poires
deh pwah
some pears

des bananes
deh ba*nan*
some bananas

des fraises
deh frez
some strawberries

des carottes
deh cah-*rott*
some carrots

des pommes
deh pom
some apples

des pommes de terre
deh pom der tair
some potatoes

de la salade
der lah sah-*lad*
some salad/lettuce

un concombre
ahn coh-*combr'*
a cucumber

des oignons
dezon-*yoh*
some onions

Je voudrais…

You are going shopping. Read the two shopping lists aloud. Start with **'je voudrais…'**. Then cut out the items you need below and fill the correct basket.

Le marché

des poires
un concombre
des tomates
des oignons
des carottes
des pommes de terre
des pommes
des fraises

Le supermarché

Can you find the purse hidden in each picture?

de la confiture
du pain
du yaourt
du shampooing
du sucre
des chips
des biscuits
du beurre

le supermarché
ler super-marsh-*eh*
supermarket

du savon
dew sav*oh*
some soap

du shampooing
dew shampoo-*eh*
some shampoo

des biscuits
deh beess-*kwee*
some biscuits

du yaourt
dew yah-*oort*
some yoghurt

des boissons
deh bwass*oh*
some drinks

du sucre
dew syookr'
some sugar

de la confiture
der lah confeet-*yoor*
some jam

du beurre
dew burr
some butter

du pain
dew pul*ı*ı
some bread

des chips
deh sheep
some crisps

un porte-monnaie
ahn port-mon-*eh*
a purse

13

Across

1 Where you would go to buy medicines.
4 Un --- trois.
5 Its coat is made into wool.
8 It is squeezed from fruit and you drink it.
9 Many people have one as a pet.
11 It shades you from the sun.
13 One.

Down

1 They are red or green and juicy.
2 Where you would go to eat out.
3 The sea is made of it.
6 Where you go to learn.
7 It is round and you play with it on the beach.
10 You spread butter on it.
12 The (two possibles).

Wordsearch

Find the French for these words, then circle them on the wordsearch. (They are all words you have already met.)

STRAWBERRIES
JAM
CRAB
FISH
SPADE
SISTER
BABY
CHOCOLATE
CUCUMBER
SOAP

14

Crossword & wordsearch

Using the words you have learnt in French, fill in this crossword. Then do the wordsearch below.
Answers on the inside cover.

C O N F I T U R E Q
H L E F P U M T R V
O I O G R O S N O S
C M P C L S O E U R
O O O M R X Y O G X
L N I F R A I S E S
A A S Z B E B E Z A
T D S O F B A E Y V
B E O D P E L L E O
C O N C O M B R E N

Spot the difference

There are eight differences between these pictures. Can you find them?
How many things can you name in French? The new words are given.

le cerf-volant
ler sair vol-*oh*

la tente
lah tont

la vache
lah vash

les bottes
leh bott

le gilet de sauvetage
ler shee-*leh* d'sowv-*taj*

le canard
ler can-*ar*

le petit canard
ler p'tee can-*ar*

la pagaie
lah pag-*eh*

le canoë
ler can-*oweh*

French fortune teller!

First colour in the four corners. Then cut out the square along the solid line. Fold back the corners along the diagonal dotted lines. Turn over (so you can read the colours and numbers) and fold back the corners again along the diagonals. Fold in half (backwards) both ways.
Now play!

bleu
bl'
beh ell er oo
blue

5 cinq

Tu seras célèbre.
too sir-a seh-lairbr'
You will be famous.

Tu seras riche.
too sir-a reesh
You will be rich.

3 trois

vert
vair er air teh
veh er air teh
green

7 sept

Tu es un cochon!
too eh ahn koshoh
You are a pig!

How to play

1. Insert the finger and thumb of each hand into the four pockets.
2. With the four corners tightly together, ask a friend to choose one of the four colours.
3. Spell out the colour in French, opening and closing the *fortune teller* each time. Use the pronunciation guide for the letters of the alphabet. *(The full A-Z is on the inside cover.)*
4. On the final letter ask your friend to select a number from inside.
5. Then count out the number in French, opening and closing as before.
6. Ask your friend to choose another number and count it out in French again.
7. Your friend selects a final number and you read the message underneath!

Tu as de la chance.
too ah der lah shah-nss
You are lucky.

6 six

Embrasse-moi!
ombrass mwah
Kiss me!

4 quatre

Tu es drôle.
too eh droll
You are funny.

2 deux

j'aune
shee
ah oo en er
shown
yellow
jaune

Tu es bête.
too eh bet
You are stupid.

1 un

Je t'aime.
sh' tem
I love you.

8 huit

rouge
roosh
air o' oo shay er
red
rouge